Resistance

Rishab Kapoor

ISBN 978-93-5610-387-0
© Rishab Kapoor 2022
Published in India 2022 by Pencil

A brand of
One Point Six Technologies Pvt. Ltd.
123, Building J2, Shram Seva Premises,
Wadala Truck Terminal, Wadala (E)
Mumbai 400037, Maharashtra, INDIA
E connect@thepencilapp.com
W www.thepencilapp.com

Author biography

Nothing is impossible if you try hard, if someone try hard dedicatedly..

CONTENTS

Preface

Things may be forget in future and vanish from our mind but truth can't be deniable and erasable. This truth may create lots aof questions and doubts but this truth also makes us proud always to be indian.

Introduction

This is a book about the struggle and sacrifice for motherland. Story of hinious and brutality of Pakistan. Without any support and positive attitude by UN and world , India conquer the war and helped Bangladesh to got indipendent.

Chapter 1

On 23 March 1971 Major Generals Khadim Hussain Raja and Rao Farman flew by helicopters and went around the cantonments outside Dhaka to personally brief the brigade commanders about the plan. They briefed Brigadiers Durrani at Jessore and Iqbal Shafi at Comilla. From Comilla Farman Ali returned to Dhaka but Khadim went to Chittagong. The situation in Chittagong was quite tricky. There was large number of Bengali troops in Chittagong. The senior most commanders there were a Bengali officer, Brig Mazumdar who was sympathetic towards Awami League. Khadim Raja told Brig Mazumdar that the troops of 2 East Bengal located at Joydevpur had shown some signs of restiveness. Therefore there was requirement of him to give a pep talk to the soldiers. He quietly told Lt Col Fatimi to assume the command in place of the brigade commander till the arrival of Brig Iqbal Shafi from Comilla. He flew Brig Mazumdar to Dhaka along with him in the helicopter. That was the end of Mazumdar's command in Pakistan Army. The other formations and unit commanders were given similar instructions by senior staff officers.11

Maj Gen Rao Farman Ali met Yahya Khan before his departure for West Pakistan. The President had planned to address the nation on 26 March on arrival at Islamabad. Rao Farman Ali prepared a draft of his speech and handed it over to Yahya Khan. The salient points of the draft speech were: (a) Mujibur Rehman should not be branded a traitor but a patriot in the hands of extremists. (b) He should not be arrested for any crime but only taken in protective custody (c) President should clearly spell out the quantum of provincial autonomy which he was prepared to give to East Pakistan. However in his speech on 26 March President Yahya Khan completely ignored the advice of Rao Farman Ali. In his address he said,...."His (Sheikh Mujib's) obstinacy, obduracy and absolute refusal to talk sense can lead to one conclusion-the man and his party is enemies of Pakistan and they want East Pakistan to break away completely which will destroy the solidarity and integrity of the country-this crime would not go unpunished." 12

A cover plan was made to deceive the Awami League leaders about Yahya Khan's departure from Dhaka. On 25 March in the evening President Yahya khan drove to Flag Staff House in the Dhaka Cantonment to have a cup of tea with Lt Gen Tikka Khan. Before the dusk the President's cavalcade drove back to the President's House with usual fanfare - pilot jeep, outriders and the president's car with star plate having four stars and his flag flying on the bonnet. But instead of Yahya Khan travelling in the car, Brig Rafiq deputized for him. But this cover plan failed in achieving the desired results as Awami League sympathizers noticed the deception. Lt Col AR Chaudhury who was on Yahya Khan's staff saw a

Dodge vehicle carrying Yahya Khan's luggage to the airport. He immediately informed Sheikh Mujibur Rehman. Yahya Khan traveled to the airport from Tikka Khan' residence incognito and entered the airport from the PAF gate. Wing Commander Khondakar saw him from his office Yahya Khan entering the airport and his plane taking off. He also informed the Awami League Chief immediately. By this time Sheikh Mujib had received warnings from other sources of the impending strike.13

The salient points of Op Searchlight were as follows. The H Hour (time for commencement of Operations) was fixed at 0100 hours on 26 March 1971. The telephone exchanges all over the province were to be switched off at 0055 hours. The commando platoon headed by Major ZA Khan tasked to arrest Sheikh Mujib was to move out at 0100hours. Movement of troops earmarked to neutralize Dhaka University and cordon off the residences of prominent citizens like Dr. Anwara Begum was to begin at 0105 hours. Curfew was to be imposed at 0110 hours, initially for 30 hours by sounding sirens and announcements made by loud speakers. Publication of news papers had to be banned till further orders. All cyclostyling machines in the University, colleges, physical training and technical institutes were to be confiscated by the army. Cut off groups had to be placed at different places to stop entry and exit from the cities during the operations. The details of troops to task were left to the brigade commanders who were to organize the task forces for specific objectives depending on their nature and the punishment which was required to be meted out to it. The unit and formation armories had to be taken over by West Pakistani troops. The weapons were issued only to West Pakistani officers. West Pakistani troop were tasked to disarm all the police stations. Units were to get hold of Ansar units. Information about Awami League leaders, student leaders, intellectuals and cultural centers, weapons catches of leftists, Awami League students' wings and ex-service-men had to be updated continuously. 14

Lt Gen Tikka Khan was the overall commander of Op Searchlight with his Tactical HQ at the Second Capital. The Province was divided in two parts for operational ease. Maj Gen Rao Farman Ali with his HQ was located at Eastern Command HQ in Dhaka was tasked to neutralize Dhaka City. He was allotted the staff of HQ Eastern Command and 57 Infantry Brigade was placed under his command. 57 Infantry Brigade had 18 and 32 Punjab Battalions, 22 Baluch, 13 Frontier force (FF) 31 Field Regiment, 13 Light Anti Aircraft Regiment and a company of commandos from 3 Commando Battalion that was located at Comilla. The tasks allotted to Farman Ali were- Neutralize by disarming 2 and 10 East Bengal and HQ East Pakistan Rifles and Reserve Police at Rajar Bagh; Capture telephone exchange, transmitters of radio and TV and State Bank of Pakistan; arrest Sheikh Mujibur Rehman and other Awami league leaders; Neutralize Iqbal Hall and Jagan Nath Hall of Dhaka University and Liaquat Hall of Engineering University; seal off the Dhaka City including entry/exit points of rail, road and river routes and protect the factory at Ghazipur and Ammunition

Depot at Rajendrapur. 15

Maj Gen Khadim Hussain Raza was the commander of 14 Infantry Division less 57 Infantry Brigade. Its allotment and tasks included-107 Infantry Brigade under command 25 and 27 Baluch Battalions, elements of 24 Field Regiment and 55 Field Regiment was in-charge of Jessore Sector. Its tasks included disarming 1 East Bengal and Sector HQ East Pakistan Rifles and Reserve Police including Ansars; secure Jessore town and the airfield and arrest Awami League and student leaders; secure telephone exchange; make Kusthia exchange operative and reinforce Khulna if need be. 22FF was tasked to secure Khulna. 23 Infantry Brigade was tasked for operations in Rangpur-Saidpur Sector and 25 Punjab for Rajshahi. For Comilla 53 Field Regiment, one and half mortar batteries, Station troops, and 3 Commando Battalion (less company) were earmarked. Their task included disarming 3 East Bengal, Wing HQ East Pakistan Rifles and Reserve District Police and securing the town and arrest of Awami League and student leaders. 31 Punjab less a company was tasked to secure Sylhet City, radio station, telephone exchange, Koeno Bridge over Surma River and disarm HQ Section of East Pakistan Rifles and Reserve Police. 16

Chittagong was considered a hard nut to be cracked. 20 Baluch less advance party with a company of 31 Punjab was ordered to move from Comilla by road and reinforce the garrison by 0100 hours on D Day. A mobile column under Brigadier Iqbal Shafi, with 24 Frontier Force, troop of heavy mortars and one field company of engineers was tasked to advance to Feni on the evening of D Day. Their task was to disarm East Bengal Regimental Center, 8 East Bengal, Sector HQ of East Pakistan Rifles and Reserve Police; Seize Central Police Armory; Secure radio station and telephone exchange; Liaise with Pakistan Navy; Liaise with CO 8 East Bengal if they felt sure of the loyalty of Bengali troops then they need not be disarmed. In that case only put up a road block so that it could ease the task of disarming of East Bengal Regimental Center and 8 East Bengal in case the troops change their loyalty. 17

Dhaka University was specially picked up because it had always been the main centre of agitations against the Government since the Language Movement. Therefore Tikka Khan decided that it must be taught a lesson which they would never forget. The University was closed during the Civil Disobedience Movement. Its hostels were partially occupied. The most important single target for the army was Sheikh Mujibur Rehman, who was the embodiment of Bengali nationalism. Therefore it was appreciated that if the Bengali nationalist movement was deprived of Sheikh Mujib's leadership, the movement would suffer a blow from which it would probably never recover.

On 25 March 1971 at 11 am Lt Gen Tikka khan telephoned Maj Gen Khadim Hussain Raja and said, "Khadim it is tonight." The Gen was already expecting the signal from MLA. He had tied up all the nitty-gritty in his Division for execution of the impending task. He summoned his senior general staff officer and passed the instructions. The general staff officers of HQ 14 Infantry Division telephoned to all the outstation garrisons and informed them the H Hour. They used the code words to pass the message. All garrisons had to act simultaneously. The orders quickly trickled down the chain of command. Hectic activities ensued in the units as soldiers got busy in drawing their weapons from the armories and ammunition from the unit magazines. Last minute-check up of automatic weapons and recoilless rifles were carried out. M-24 tanks of 29 Cavalry were moved to Dhaka from Rangpur for Op Searchlight. The tank crew got busy oiling the tracks and cleaning the gun barrels of the World War II vintage machines. 18 The troops had to be in the vicinity of the objective before H hour i.e. 0100 hours. Some of the units and sub units had started their move at 11.30 pm on 25 March considering the road blocks established by the Awami League supporters. The first column of troops moving out of the Dhaka Cantonment met resistance at the Farm Gate, about one kilometer from their start point. There was a roadblock which was created by felling a huge tree across the road. The side gaps were covered with hulks of old cars and a disabled steamroller. On the city side of the road block there were several hundred Awami League supporters shouting Joi Bangla slogans. Very soon some rifle shots mingled with the slogans. Soon thereafter burst of automatic weapons fire shrilled through the atmosphere. The process of firing and shouting of slogans continued for some time which was punctuated by chatter of light and medium machine guns' fire. After some time the slogans started dying down and firing began to subside. Most of the slogan shouters were gunned down. The weapon had triumphed albeit temporarily in silencing the voice of liberty. The action had begun before the H hour. There was no point now in sticking to the laid down H hour and TIkka Khan gave a go ahead signal to pursue the operations relentlessly. 19

The date of D Day for launch of Op Searchlight, 26 March 1971 was decided by Yahya Khan to coincide with the second anniversary of his assumption of power as the second military dictator of Pakistan. As soon as the President's aircraft was fully airborne and signs of tightening of seat belts were switched off, the waiter appeared in front him and asked what drink the President would like to have? Yahya Khan ordered for his favorite Scotch whisky with soda. A big party was waiting for him at Karachi to celebrate the second anniversary of his becoming the President. He was enjoying his Scotch and soda and snacks while cruising at an altitude of 40,000 feet above mean sea level over Sri Lanka when the captain of the aircraft appeared in front him and after saluting informed him that Op Searchlight had begun. 20 He took a long sip of whisky and mulled over the prospects of his enjoying power in Pakistan, without any interference, for an indefinite period of time. He had no doubts about the outcome of the operations in the Eastern Wing since he had assigned the task of sorting out the Bengalis to the most competent General for such jobs. After all it was Tikka Khan who had massacred thousands of innocent Baluchis and had earned the sobriquet of "Bomber of Baluchistan." Yahya Khan had let loose an experienced hawk to hunt the hapless birds in Bangladesh. As the President de-boarded the aircraft at Karachi airport in an inebriated state past mid-night on 26 March, thousands of people of had already been massacred and the province was burning.

Pakistan Army secured the desired objectives in Dhaka by first light of 26 March 1971 but Bengali fighters located in Chittagong, Rajshahi and Pabna and some other towns gave them quite a tough time for several days. In Chittagong there were about 5000 Bengali troops as compared to 600 West Pakistanis. Among the Bengali troops 2500 were trained recruits of East Bengal Regimental Center. Then there were troops of newly raised 8 East Bengal, East Pakistan Rifles Wing and Sector HQ besides the police. The West Pakistani troops were mainly from 20 Baluch whose advance party had already left for the Western Wing. A senior non-Bengali officer Lt Col Fatimi was given the command of the Chittagong garrison by Maj Gen Khadim when he had flown the commander Brig Mazumdar two days earlier to Dhaka. 21 Tension in Chittagong had been building for over couple of days before the launch of Op Searchlight. The Awami League leaders of Chittagong came to know about talks being stalled on 25 March and Pakistan Army's preparations for the crackdown. The same evening Awami League leaders assembled at the residence of MR Siddiqui to take stock of the situation. They got in touch with Capt Rafiqul Islam 'to take appropriate action.' 22 Rafiqul Islam was in favor of taking preemptive action against the Pakistani forces in and around Chittagong while they were still relatively weak. He had even discussed this idea on the previous day with two senior Bengali officers, Lt Col MR Chaudhury of the East Bengal Regimental Centre (EBRC) and Maj Ziaur Rehman of the 8 East Bengal Regiment. Both these officers refused and advised him to 'stop his men from taking immediate action.' 21

But the Capt did not listen to the senior officers' advice. On being encouraged by the local Awami League leaders, Rafiqul Islam started arresting the West Pakistanis in the East Pakistan Rifles lines and secured the armory. In the meantime Major Ziaur Rehman was proceeding towards Chittagong Port to get the ammunition unloaded from Pakistani Ship MV Swat as per the orders of his superior (Pakistani) officers. Because the Bangladeshi labor had already refused to unload the ship on the call of Sheikh Mujbur Rehman therefore Major Zia was ordered to perform this task. As Major Zia was dutifully proceeding to the port to perform the task assigned to him when Pakistani troops suddenly attacked the Bengali soldiers of EBRC at 11.30 p.m. when they were in their beds. Taken by surprise many of them including Lt Col MR Chaudhury were killed. Some troops of EBRC managed to escape East Bengal unit barracks and saved themselves. When another Bengali officer, Capt Khalikuzzaman heard about this incident he immediately rushed to inform Ziaur Rehman and warned him that if he proceeded to the jetty as per orders his own life could be in danger.

Ziaur Rehman immediately rushed to his unit which was composed almost entirely of the Bengali troops and including large number of officers. In the meantime the escapees from EBRC were requesting 8 EBR to come to the rescue of EBRC troops and their families. But Ziaur Rehman consulted his officers and decided against their request as it would have been too risky. Thereafter Ziaur Rehman ordered his troops to kill all the Pakistani officers. He also ordered his unit to move to Paitya and later crossed the river and reached Kalurghat. Capt Rafiqul Islam was left alone to fight in Chittagong. If Major Ziaur Rehman had organized the defenses on a strong point based on the built up area then he could have kept the Pakistanis at bay for a considerable time and would have inflicted very heavy casualties on them. 22

As per the operational plan Brig Iqbal Shafi advanced from Comilla towards Chittagong with his mobile column. But his advance was stalled by the Bangladeshi troops at the Feni Bridge. The GOC Maj Gen Khadim came to know about the stoppage at 0050 on 26 March. He ordered Brig Iqbal to cross the ravine and leave the bridge in the Hostiles' hands and move forward to Chittagong at the earliest. But Brig Shafi could not make any headway without taking the bridge which his column could capture only at 10 a.m. After capturing the bridge the column resumed its advance but was again pinned down by Bangladesh troops at Cameera, about 20 kilometers short of Chittagong. The commanding officer of 24 Frontier Force and 11 soldiers were killed in the battle. The mobile column also lost wireless contact with Brigade

HQ at Comilla and the HQ of 14 Infantry Division at Dhaka. All sorts of apprehensions were aired about the mobile column under Brig Iqbal Shafi in absence of communications. Was it butchered! If so what would happen to the Chittagong garrison and what about the fate of Operation Searchlight if the city was not captured? These were the anxieties expressed by the senior officers in Dhaka. 23

On 27 March Gen Khadim Raja decided to locate the column of Brig Shafi himself. He decided to fly by helicopter to Chittagong first and then follow the Chittagong-Comilla Road to locate the column where it was struck. As his helicopter tried to land close to Chittagong Hills in 20 Baluch area, it drew fire from the Bangladeshi troops who had taken up positions on the nearby high ground. The helicopter was hit by the bullets but the damage was not serious. It managed to land safely. The General got a quick briefing from Lt Col Fatimi on the situation in Chittagong. He reported to him about the capture of EBRC in which 50 Bangladeshi soldiers were killed and 500 arrested. Fatimi told the General that the remaining city of Chittagong was still in the hands of Bangladeshis. Khadim Raja again took off in his helicopter and resumed the flight along the Comilla road. However he could not locate the column of Brig Iqbal Shafi due to low cloud formation. The General was carrying out continuous study of his quarter inch map. On nearing Cameera he ordered the pilots to cut through the cloud cover and fly low. As the helicopter lowered down Khadim craned out his neck from the window of his flying machine. A quick burst of bullets was fired on the chopper from the ground below. The pilots quickly pulled up the machine. However it was hit by one bullet which pierced through its belly missing the fuel tank by a few inches. Khadim ordered the pilots to fly back to Dhaka. 24

In the meantime Gen AO Mitha sent a detachment of 3 Commando Battalion from Dhaka by air to Chittagong to link up with the Iqbal Shafi's column. The detachment did not know the ground position of the missing column or that of the Bangladeshi troops. In the meantime a Bengali officer, Capt Hamid met the CO of the Commando Battalion and told him, "I have come from Murree to look up my parents in Chittagong. I know the area. May I go with you as a guide?" The CO promptly accepted his request. On 27 March the Commando Battalion undertook the search/link up operations. Major General Khadim moved his tactical HQ to Chittagong area. He sent a column of 20 Baluch from Chittagong on the link up mission from another approach than the Chittagong-Comilla Road. This column was heavily fired at by Bangladeshi troops and could not make any headway. But the column of Commando Battalion moved quite fast due to the Guidance provided by the Bengali officer Capt Hamid. As they were moving on Chittagong-Comilla Road they drew intensive fire from the flanking hills and suffered heavy casualties. The CO, two captains, one junior commissioned officer and nine other ranks were killed. 25

In the meantime Brig Iqbal Shafi assumed the command of the mobile column after the death of the CO of 24 FF. A battery of mortars had also joined the mobile column. Shafi's column closed on to the defenses of Bangladesh forces along the Chittagong-Comilla Road. He launched a dawn attack on 28 March which managed to clear the axis. This cleared his way to Chittagong and he reached Haji Camp, the resting place for pilgrims, which was on the edge of Chittagong city. On 29 March the link up of all the three columns took place and Chittagong was finally captured by Pakistan Army. The next objective for the Pakistan Army was the concentration of Bangladeshi troops around Kalurghat transmitter of Radio Pakistan, which was being used as Bangladesh Betar Kendra. The transmitter building was very well fortified with pillboxes and foxholes. The defenses were nicely interconnected with communication trenches. Major General Mitha's commandos were tasked to clear the area. He sent a commando detachment to blow up the transmitter. The commando detachment approached the target area from a flank following the river route in country oats. They came under extensive fire from the Bangladeshi troops while they were still in the boats. Sixteen commandos were killed. General Mitha made another attempt to capture the transmitter but his troops suffered very heavy casualties. Major General Khadim Raja sent a column of 20 Baluch under Lt Col Fatimi. These troops also drew very heavy fire from Bangladeshi troops and failed to make any headway. Finally two US supplied F-86s Sabres of Pakistan Air Force were pressed into service which knocked out the Kalurghat defenses. The next objective was East Pakistan Rifles HQ where about 1000 Bangladeshi troops were entrenched. The Bangladeshi troops had sited their defenses on a high ground along an embankment. On 31 March the Pakistan Army launched an attack with an infantry battalion supported by a naval destroyer, two gun boats, two tanks and a heavy mortar battery. The Bangladeshi troops fought valiantly but due to superior enemy armaments and numerical superiority they were subdued after three hours of high intensity battle. There after Pakistan Army launched the attack on the Reserve Police Lines where 20,000 rifles were stocked. A battalion size attack was launched on the Reserve Police Lines. After putting a fight for some time they withdrew to Kaptai and most them crossed over to India later. The main operations were over by 31 March but the mopping up continued till 6 April. 26

The Pakistan Army faced the biggest odds in Kushtia and Pabna. Pakistanis did not have any troops permanently located in Kushtia. On 26 March a company of 27 Baluch was sent to Kushtia with the task of guarding important government installations and to enforce curfew and collect arms and ammunition from the civilians. The company commander distributed the troops accordingly in small detachments. The detachments were tasked to guard the telephone exchange and the VHF station. The company commander sent some parties to arrest the local Awami League leaders but they all had vanished. He killed some innocent civilians to make his presence felt. "On 28 March at about 9.30 pm. the local superintendent of police, pale with fear, came to the company commander, Major Shoaib, and reported that rebels had gathered in the border town of Chaudanga, about 16 kilometers from Kushtia and were planning to attack the town at night. They were also threatening to kill all 'collaborators.' The company commander passed a word of caution to his platoons. But the troops did not take it seriously. They did not even dig the trenches. The Bangladeshi attack commenced at 3.45 a.m. (29 March) with heavy mortar shelling. …They (Pakistani Troops) soon realized that the attacker were none other than the troops of 1st Bengal which had been sent out from Jessore Cantonment by (Indian) Border Security Force (BSF) (Four Indian BSF soldiers were captured near Jessore and two near Sylhet) Their first objective was the police armory which was occupied by the Pakistanis. The Bangladeshi troops climbed the roof top of the three storied building which was the residence of the District Judge. They used this building as a platform and sprayed the police armory with bullets. By the dawn of 29 Match five Pakistani soldiers were killed. The toll of the Pakistani soldiers killed by Bangladesh forces rose to eleven by 9 am and twenty by 10 am. Only a few survivors could manage to escape to the company HQ which was about a kilometer away. The Bangladeshis simultaneously attacked the Pakistani troops at the telephone exchange and the VHF station. In the company HQ twenty five Pakistani troops were killed. The company commander sent frantic messages to higher HQ for help and also requested for an air strike. But the message by the end of the day was gloomy which said, "Troops here are already committed. No reinforcement possible. Air strike called off due to poor visibility…Khuda Hafiz!" 27

The company commander collected the survivors. When he carried out the head count he noticed that only 65 out 125 had survived. He lined up 3 xthree tons and 1xone ton vehicles and six jeeps. The convoy marched towards Jessore. They had travelled 25 kilometers from Kusthia when the leading two jeeps caved into a culvert. The Bangladeshi troops had laid an ambush for them. They had cut the culvert on the Kushtia-Jessore Road in the center and camouflaged it nicely so that the breach was not noticed. The leading jeeps, including that of Major Shohaib, plunged in to the drain below the culvert. Bangladeshis opened very intense fire on the halted convoy. Only nine out of the sixty five could survive and crawled out of the ambush site. They managed to escape but some of them were apprehended by the freedom fighters that put them to death. 28

In Pabna the Pakistani forces met the same fate at the hands of Bangladeshi troops. A company of 25 Punjab consisting of 130 all ranks under Capt Asghar was sent to Pabna from Rajshahi to establish the presence of the Pakistani forces in the area and to guard the vital installations. The company carried only the first line ammunition and light weapons since they thought that they were going only for internal security duties. On arrival in Pabna the company was divided in small detachments for guarding the vital installations like the power house and the telephone exchange. The troops went to the houses of local Awami League leaders but found them missing. They consolidated their positions on 26 March but on 27 March at about 6 pm all the company detachments came under intensive fire from the Bangladeshi forces. The freedom fighters force comprised of 900 hundred troops of the East PakistanRrifles Wing, 30 Police personnel and 40 Awami League volunteers. Capt Asghar made an attempt to dislodge the freedom fighters. He along with a platoon attacked the freedom fighters but received a burst from a Bangladeshi light machine gun. He died on the spot. Another attempt was made by the company second-in- command lieutenant Rashid who was also killed on the spot. There after all the detachments wound up except one at the telephone exchange. The Bangladeshi forces launched an all out attack on the Pakistanis. In the battle Pakistanis had lost two officers, three junior commissioned officers and eighty other ranks. One more officer and thirty two other ranks were wounded. The company sent frantic SOS calls for reinforcements. One helicopter came to evacuate the wounded soldiers but could not land. Major Aslam from Rajshahi along with eighteen other ranks managed to reach Pabna with one recoilless rifle, one machine gun and some ammunition and managed to extricate the survivors. He loaded the wounded in a dodge vehicle and sent them to Rajshahi across country to avoid any possibility of being intercepted en-route. There after he took the able bodied along with him to fight his way to Rajshahi by road. He met very heavy resistance on the way and took to the cross countryside where they wandered for three days without food or water. When the column ultimately reached Rajshahi on 1 April at 10 am, only eighteen soldiers were counted, the remaining including Major Aslam had been killed by the Bangladeshi forces. Chittagong, Kushtia and Pabna were the main positions, where the Bangladeshis gave the most relentless fight to the Pakistanis. These places were taken over by the Pakistanis on 6, 16 and 10 April respectively. 29 In Joydebpur 2 East Bengal located in the old palace building had a sprinkling of officers, Junior Commissioned Officers; and Non Commissioned Officers, from West Pakistan. The battalion revolted on 28 March once they learnt about the massacre of innocent Bangladeshis from mid night of 26 March. They killed all the West Pakistanis. When a company of Punjab Regiment was sent to quell the rebellion the Bengalis escaped with weapons and ammunition. Similar incidents took place at different locations.

Once the major towns were cleared the Pakistan army started moving to the country side. They adopted the same scorched earth policy. Strong columns of the troops went to the smaller towns and the villages. Brig Siddiq Salik has described the scenes of some of these operations in his book 'Witness to the surrender' of a column from Dhaka to Tangail on 1 April which he had accompanied. "The main column moved on the main road. The troops in vehicles had their machine guns fitted ready to bring automatic fire on the enemy. Two companies were spread five hundred meters astride the road in field formations as per the military battle proceedures for advance to contact with enemy. Behind the infantry columns was a battery of field guns which fired a few shells at suitable intervals in the direction of their move in order to scare away the Bangladeshis. The infantry columns opened fire at the slightest pretext or mere suspicion. The stir in a bunch of trees or a little rustle in the bari (house) was enough to evoke a burst of automatic fire or at least a rifle shot. ... a little short of Karatea, on the Tangail road, there was small locality which hardly rated any name. The searching troops passed through it, putting a match to thatched huts and the adjoining bamboo plants. As soon as they advanced ahead a bamboo stick burst with a crack because of the heat of the fire. Everybody took it as a rifle shot by the hidden 'miscreants.' This caused the weight of the entire column to be riveted on the locality and all sorts of weapons fired into the trees. When the column commander was sure that the source of the danger had been eliminated a careful search was ordered. The search party found no sign of human being alive or dead. The sound of bamboo burst had delayed the march...." 30

Appendix

A must read book...

List of Contributors

A book with many unreveal history till date

Notes

R P Singh (VSM) Brigadier

Hitesh Singh

Rishab Kapoor

Kaushal Hingu